DEATH VALLEY

A VISUAL
INTERPRETATION

With an Essay
by
JEFF NICHOLAS

DEATH VALLEY

A VISUAL
INTERPRETATION

Carpet of Desertgold & the Grapevine Mountains

Badlands near Zabriskie Point.

The Watchtower at Scottys Castle.

FRONT COVER: Badlands near Zabriskie Point.
BACK COVER: Manly Beacon at dawn seen from Zabriskie Point.

ISBN O-939365-37-5

Printed in Singapore.
First Edition 1994.

ACKNOWLEDGEMENTS

We would like to take this opportunity to thank the many photographers who made their imagery available to us during the editing of this title. While no single image can effectively replace the actual experience of being there, we believe the visual story told by the images contained in this volume do tell the story of seasonal change and process more effectively than what the visitor would experience while on vacation. On behalf of those who will see this book, we thank you for sharing the fruits of your labors.

We would also like to thank those members of the Death Valley Natural History Association and the National Park Service whose assistance has been invaluable in the creation and formation of this book—Thank You!

DEDICATION

This book is a visual tribute to the insight of those few who saw the wisdom of setting aside such a tract of land for the future, without regard for personal gain. That Death Valley and the National Park Service have become models for more than 130 countries from around the world is all the proof that is necessary to confirm their wisdom. We can only hope our own use is consistent with this wisdom and in no way contributes to the degradation of this most extraordinary legacy.

In this spirit, let us all pledge to continue to work, and sacrifice, for the greater good of places such as Death Valley.

SIERRA PRESS, INC.

4988 Gold Leaf Drive, Mariposa, CA 95338

CONTENTS

The Valley of Life

by
Jeff Nicholas

It is probably safe to assume that the first white visitors to Death Valley were not overly impressed by their introduction to this portion of western Nevada and eastern California. Horrified is probably more accurate. This group of emigrants, following what they believed to be a shortcut to the gold fields of California, must surely have stood in awe when they arrived at the mouth of Furnace Creek Wash on Christmas Day, 1849. Before them lay not what they so desperately needed—a green, water-fed valley that would provide forage for their oxen and meat for the cook pot; instead, they saw a sight quite unlike anything they had seen before.

A vast depression lay before them, stretching to the north and south as far as the eye could see, and bounded on the west by a great mountain range (the Panamints) rising more than two vertical miles above the valley floor. In the bottom of the valley lay not the cottonwood-lined river or willow-bordered lake they hoped for, but rather, a great expanse of salt and mud and sand.

Having already traversed hundreds of miles of desert in western

Nevada, they had little idea of just where they were. They believed the sleepy village of Los Angeles must surely lie just beyond the next mountain range. In truth, they were still at least 150 miles northeast of there (as the raven flies). The green, spring-fed meadows of Las Vegas, which would have provided the water and forage they needed, lay roughly 100 miles east of them. This group of 49ers (as they are now known) had unwittingly discovered the hottest, driest, and lowest place on the North American continent.

HOTTEST, DRIEST, LOWEST

Death Valley is one of the hottest places on earth—if not *the* hottest. Daytime temperatures during the summer routinely exceed 120 degrees Fahrenheit, with ground temperatures regularly rising as much as 50 percent higher. The highest reading on record in the park is 134 degrees, which occurred July 10, 1913 at Furnace Creek. It is probable that the temperature was several degrees higher at Badwater—20 miles south of Furnace Creek and nearly 100 feet lower—it usually is. This means the highest temperature ever recorded on earth—136 degrees at Azizia, Libya—was probably bested by Badwater on that day in 1913.

Heat, aridity, and elevation come together in Death Valley to create an environment of extreme intensity—one that lies at the very edge of human endurance. Death Valley is in the rainshadow of several parallel mountain ranges: the Sierra Nevada and the White, Argus,

Pressure ridges in the salt pan near Badwater.

and Panamint mountain ranges. The Sierra Nevada, with a crestline of 10,000 to 14,000 feet, effectively drains the moisture out of most winter storms. Whatever precipitation gets past the Sierra Nevada is usually deposited on the White, Argus, or Panamint ranges. Snow depths of up to twenty feet are not uncommon on Telescope Peak—the highest elevation in the Panamints and the park—during the winter months. By the time storms reach Death Valley they are so weak that the average "winter" rainfall at Furnace Creek during the months of November to February is less than one inch.

During the summer heated air rising from the floor of Death Valley usually prevents rain from reaching the valley. The moisture is either blown back up into the sky by the force of the rising air, or the heat causes the rain to evaporate before it can reach the ground. The sight of long, silvery strands of rain disappearing in mid-air—known as "virga"—is not uncommon.

Although summer storms have little effect on the valley floor, higher elevations in the park typically receive greater precipitation (an additional two-thirds of an inch per thousand feet of elevation gained). It is here that summer rains have their greatest impact. Cloudbursts drop large volumes of water on small areas. Because the rocky, exposed landscape of Death Valley cannot absorb much moisture, rapid run-off and flashfloods are common. These powerful surges of water either carve deep pathways through soft sedimentary rock—as seen at Zabriskie Point or in Golden Canyon near Furnace Creek—or contribute to the formation of massive alluvial fans—such as those that appear to nearly swallow the base of the Panamints along the west side of the valley. These vast alluvial fans are the result of erosion and are composed of sediments deposited at the base of the mountains by the force of running water. The volume of alluvium is even greater than it appears: scientists estimate that the floor of Death Valley is actually the top of 8,000 to 10,000 feet of sediments that have been eroded from the surrounding mountains. These processes are ongoing and continue to reshape the landscape with each new storm.

Another factor contributing to the heat and low humidity is solar radiation. With more than 300 days of brilliant sunshine per year, the rate of evaporation is much greater than the available precipitation. Some estimates place this evaporative rate at nearly 150 inches per year, in an area that typically receives less than two inches of rainfall. This evaporation rate also affects plants and animals (including human visitors). The denizens of this landscape have evolved over a long period of time, coming up with any number of ingenious adaptations; most visitors, on the other hand, have not. When in Death Valley, drink water—lots of it.

The final factor of import in the heat-humidity formula has to do with

Sunrise on the dunes at Mesquite Flat.

the fact that Death Valley is the lowest place in the western hemisphere—dipping to 282 feet below sea level a few miles northwest of Badwater (which is 279.8 feet below sea level). As heated air rises from the floor of the valley it draws in air from the higher elevations that surround it. The air must descend thousands of feet, and as it descends it gets hotter—Furnace Creek hot!

Why is Death Valley so low? In a nutshell, the bottom fell out. By some 35 million years ago, this entire region of eastern California and western Nevada had been fractured by seismic forces associated with plate tectonics, or continental drift. These fractures (or faults, as they are more properly known) parallel one another and are responsible for the Basin and Range topography of this part of North America. Following this initial fracturing, beginning some 35 million years ago, powerful forces from deep in the earth uplifted, tilted, and folded much of this region. During this period, which lasted some 30 million years, huge blocks of the earth's surface either rose or fell along these faults. In the case of Death Valley, the Panamint, Grapevine, Funeral, and Black mountains all rose. The block that now supports the floor of the valley (remember, there are 8,000 to 10,000 feet of sediments resting atop this block) fell relative to the blocks that form the mountainous "walls" of the valley.

Over the course of the last 35 million years, in addition to these changes in the shape of the land, the environment of Death Valley has seen many changes as well. At one time or another this region has been inundated by oceans, flooded by lakes that were filled with glacial run-off from the Sierra Nevada following several ice ages, and lastly, it has been baked by the seemingly relentless heat the visitor experiences today. These processes of change, be they to the landscape or the environment, are continuing today. Flashfloods reconfigure canyon floors and deposit new material at the tops of alluvial fans; the eastern side of Death Valley continues to drop along the fault at the base of the Black Mountains; the availability of groundwater is affected by seismic activity; and ephemeral pools filled with rainwater provide for the needs of wildlife and deposit new minerals wherever, and whenever, they form. Occasionally, these minerals "paint" the landscape as they break down, or oxidize. Artists Palette, at the base of the Black Mountains south of Furnace Creek, is a fabulous jumble of color: reds, oranges, and browns (iron); purples and violets (manganese); and greens (mica) blend together, creating a kaleidoscope of color.

EARLY INHABITANTS
Despite its harsh and seemingly uninhabitable appearance, Death Valley has been home to Native American cultures for nearly 10,000

years. Archeologists have identified four distinct cultures.

The first of these, the Nevares Spring People (or Death Valley I), lived here at least 9,000 years ago, at a time when lakes filled with post-Ice Age glacial run-off from the Sierra Nevada would still have existed on the floor of the valley. They were hunter-gatherers who probably lived in Death Valley year-round. The firepits and semicircular stone shelters they built have been found near fresh-water springs on the gravel alluvial terraces of the valley. Most of these springs dried up long ago, as the environment of Death Valley became more arid following the last Ice Age (about 10,000 years ago.) The changing climate may have affected the environment in such a way as to lead to the disappearance of this culture.

The Nevares Spring People were succeeded, roughly 5,000 years ago, by the Mesquite Flat People (or Death Valley II). Like the Nevares people, they were hunter-gatherers. They lived (probably year-round) along the perimeter of the valley's salt pan at a time when freshwater springs were more abundant than they are today. In addition to the circles of stones and firepits they left, projectile points, stone knives, choppers, and seed grinding stones are also found in and around their homesites. Most archeologists feel this indicates an increased knowledge, and use, of plant by-products in their diet. As the environment here continued to

evolve, the springs these people relied on likely dried up, leading to their migration elsewhere.

The next group of inhabitants were the Saratoga Spring People (Death Valley III). By the time these people arrived, about 2,000 years ago, Death Valley probably appeared much as it does today. Gone were the Ice Age lakes and freshwater springs, which supported grasses, trees, and wildlife. Despite this increased harshness (or perhaps because of it?) the Saratoga Spring People were a much more advanced hunting and gathering culture than their predecessors. They used bows and arrows, rather than the atlatl (an effective but none-theless primitive spear-throwing device). Arrow and point sizes were determined by the size of their prey (from rabbits and rodents to bighorn sheep). The relatively large number of grinding stones found at their sites implies an even greater knowledge, and use, of seeds than their predecessors had. In addition to the charms, pendants, figurines, and beads with which they adorned themselves (and which imply far-reaching trade routes across the Southwest), they also created patterns, lines, and geometric shapes with which they adorned the landscape. These earthworks, some up to thirty feet in diameter, were composed of cobblestones meticulously laid out on hand-cleared gravel slopes. The function of these earthworks is not known—perhaps they were ceremonial, perhaps

Playa forming in a small crater near Ubehebe Crater.

not. Little is known of these early cultures. Hopefully, further archeological research will reveal more details of their lifestyles and histories.

The last culture identified by archeologists was living here when the 49ers passed through. This final group (Death Valley IV) are known as the Desert Shoshone and they still call Death Valley home. They were nomadic hunters and gatherers who began arriving here on seasonal migrations about a thousand years ago. Camping near springs on the valley floor during the winter months (their largest village was near present-day Furnace Creek), they hunted bighorn sheep, wove nets and built rock deadfalls to trap small game, and gathered pinyon nuts, mesquite beans, and grass seeds when ripe. Summer months were spent in the cooler temperatures of the mountains. Today, however, with modern conveniences such as air conditioning, many members of the Timbisha Shoshone Tribe reside at Furnace Creek year round.

THE RECENT PAST
That first group of lost visitors to Death Valley—about one hundred people—were looking for a shortcut to the gold fields of California. After the initial shock and disappointment of not finding the food, water, and forage they so desperately had hoped for had worn off, they decided to split into two groups.

The first of these, the "Jayhawkers," was made up of seventy to eighty people, mostly young, single men from the Midwest. They headed north and west toward the north end of Tucki Mountain. Near the site of the Devils Cornfield and Mesquite Flat Sand Dunes (close to present-day Stovepipe Wells Village), they burnt their wagons in order to smoke the meat from the last of their oxen. They left Death Valley by way of Townes Pass with, apparently, little undue suffering or hardship.

The second group did not fare so well. They were forced to stop near the base of the Panamint Mountains when their draft animals gave out, most likely at Tule Spring. From here, they sent William Manly and John Rogers to seek help. When the two young men finally returned, some four weeks later, they found only the Bennett and Arcane families remaining. With the exception of Captain Robert Culverwell, who was found dead of exposure, the whereabouts of the others who struck out on their own when Manly and Rogers failed to return quickly is unknown. Folklore has it that it was one of the women in the Bennett-Arcane group who muttered "Goodbye, Death Valley," as they crested the Panamints on their way to safety, thus naming what had previously been terra incognita for most Americans.

While the Bennett-Arcane group was responsible for affixing the name by which we know this valley today, it was the Jayhawkers who would ultimately have the greatest impact. It seems that while leaving Death Valley a member of that group picked up a rock to use as a replacement for his lost gunsight. This piece of rock would later be assayed as almost pure silver ore. This touched off nearly a century of boom-bust mining operations that can still be seen today at sites such as Skidoo, Rhyolite, the Keane Wonder Mine, Chloride City, the Charcoal Kilns in Wildrose Canyon, Ashford Mill, and the Harmony & Eagle Borax Works.

These early prospectors and explorers also filled history books with such colorful names as Shorty Harris, One-eyed Thompson, "Twenty Mule Team," and , of course, Death Valley Scotty— whose unlikely friendship with the reclusive Chicago multimillionaire Albert M. Johnson resulted in the construction of the Spanish provincial-style hacienda known today as Scotty's Castle.

Begun in 1922, this "castle," which is located in Grapevine Canyon at the northern end of Death Valley, eventually grew to more than 31,000 square feet and includes guest houses, stables, a pipe organ, indoor fountains, a 185-foot pool, a 56-foot "chime-tower," and 120,000 railroad ties for firewood. Sadly, the "castle" was never completed as construction was halted in 1931 when Johnson's wealth was affected by the Great Depression.

In the early 1920s the first "tourist-camp" in Death Valley—actually only tent houses—was installed near the site of present-day Stovepipe Wells Village. In 1927, Furnace Creek Ranch opened to the public, when a borax company converted its buildings into a resort. Furnace Creek Inn, spectacularly situated at the mouth of Furnace Creek Wash, was built and opened at about the same time. In 1933, with visitation growing as it became a popular winter destination, nearly 3,000 square miles of the California-Nevada desert was set aside, and Death Valley National Monument came into existence (see page 13 for information concerning the efforts currently underway to establish Death Valley National Park).

LIVING WITH THE LAND

At first glance, it appears that there is hardly a living thing inhabiting the floor of Death Valley. And, in some areas, that is absolutely true. But what Death Valley may lack in density of life, it more than makes up for in diversity.

The great range of elevations found in the park— from 282 feet below sea level near Badwater to 11,049 feet atop Telescope Peak—contributes significantly to this diversity. This is, after all, the equivalent of travelling from the Equator to the Arctic Circle. Within the park's bounds nearly 1,000 plant species have been identified—from pickleweed and grasses at Badwater to limber and bristlecone pines atop the Panamints. This list also includes thirty grasses, fifteen cacti, ten ferns, six lilies—including the magnificent Joshua tree—and two

Desert flora growing on the wall of Titus Canyon.

species of orchids that grow nowhere else on earth. In all, there are twenty different endemic species in the park.

In addition to this wealth of plant life, nearly 500 species of vertebrates have been identified as inhabiting the park at least seasonally. Of these, roughly 350 are birds—not only golden eagles, peregrine falcons, and the ubiquitous ravens but snipes, sandpipers, numerous ducks, and even great blue herons. There are roughly three dozen species of reptiles, including desert tortoises, a multitude of lizards (geckos, iguanas, and chuckawallas, to name but a few), as well as numerous snakes—boas, whipsnakes, gopher snakes, kingsnakes, the Panamint rattlesnake, the Mojave Desert sidewinder, and even four toads. There are nearly five dozen mammal species, many of which are mice, rats, gophers, and ground squirrels; however, the list also includes desert bighorn sheep, mountain lions, badgers, coyotes, kit foxes, bobcats, mule deer, and even pronghorns.

What all these plant and animal species have in common is that they have all devised survival strategies that are consistent with their environment. For some animals this is a matter of migrating seasonally to higher or lower elevations (mule deer, bighorn sheep, and feral burros, to name a few). Others wait out the heat and exposure of midday in favor of a nocturnal life (coyote, kit fox, and most lizards).

Still others will simply hunker down and wait for the optimum conditions—as when toads estivate (a state of torpor resembling hibernation).

Desert plants, too, have evolved their own sets of strategies for dealing with the conditions they must endure. Some of these are surprisingly similar to those of the animal kingdom—nocturnal blooming cycles and going to seed to wait for the next good rain, as with annual wildflowers, are two good examples. Others have evolved waxy leaves that restrict evaporation or turn away from the sun (creosote bush), and still others are capable of sending their roots fifty to sixty feet beneath the surface, as does the mesquite tree.

While we may refer to the environment of Death Valley as being harsh, inhospitable, unforgiving, and uninhabitable, for the denizens of this landscape, it is simply "home." In all likelihood, the environment you call home, and therefore are comfortable in, would be harsh and uninhabitable to these desert-adapted species. We should take care not to disturb their lives by extending to them the same consideration and respect we do to others of our own species. After all, to these residents, this is not a valley of death—it is the Valley of Life.

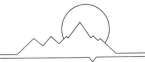

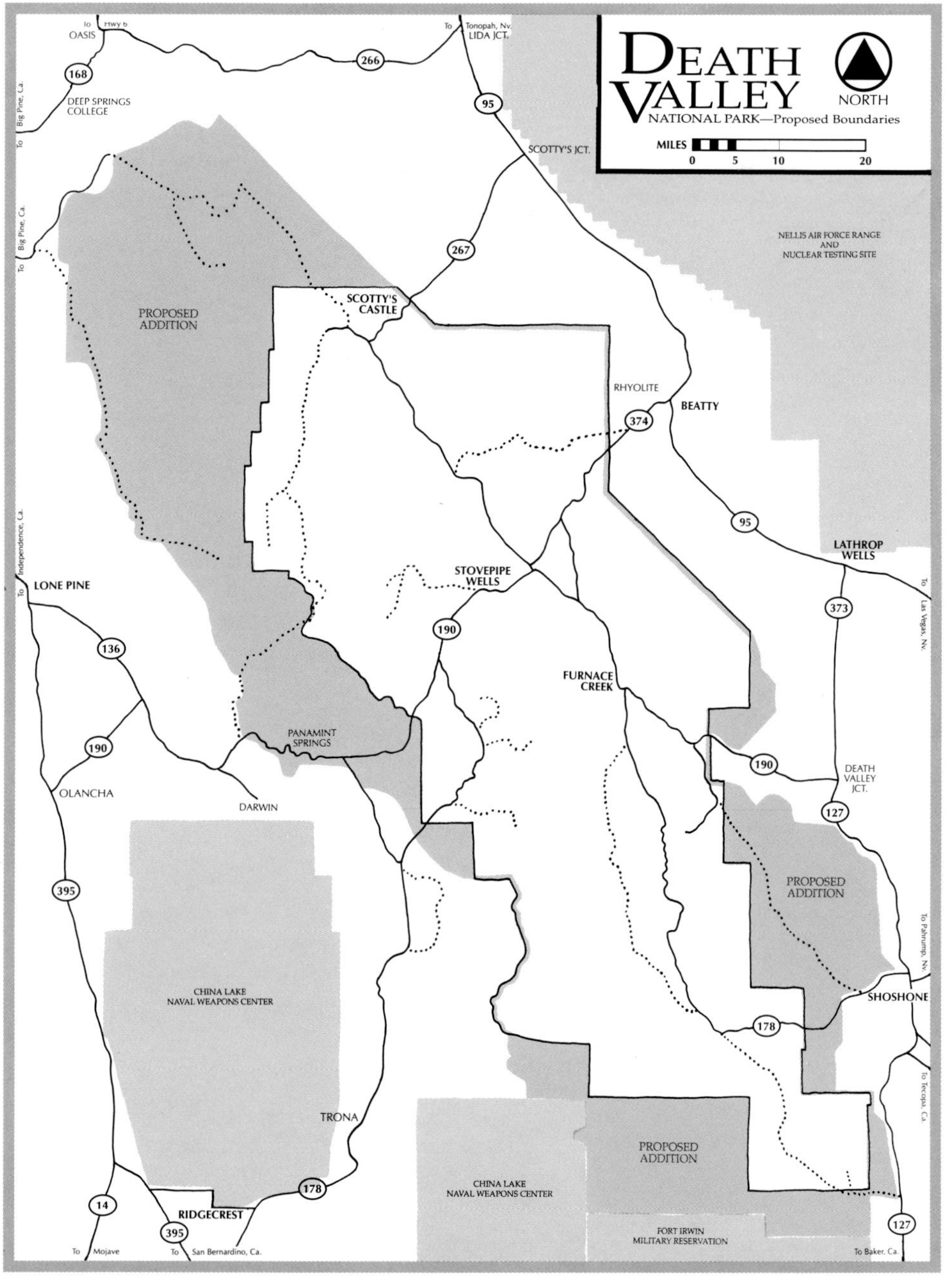

DEATH VALLEY
NATIONAL PARK—Proposed Boundaries

NORTH

MILES
0   5   10   20

The CALIFORNIA DESERT PROTECTION ACT of 1993/94

On January 21, 1993, legislation was introduced in the U.S. Congress by California Senators Feinstein and Boxer which would re-designate Death Valley and Joshua Tree national monuments as National Parks as well as establish a new Mojave National Park in the region currently administered by the Bureau of Land Management as the East Mojave Scenic Area.

In addition to these name and administrative changes, this legislation would also add acreage to both existing monuments. Joshua Tree would be enlarged by approximately 234,000 acres (to ~800,000 acres) and Death Valley would be expanded by roughly 1.3 million acres, increasing its size to 3.3 million acres (see map at left—red areas are the proposed additions). The new Mojave National Park would occupy roughly 1.2 million acres.

All three of these actions will provide additional—much needed— protection of habitat for the 635 vertebrate and 700 flowering plant species that inhabit the California desert.

This Bill (S.21), as of this writing in May 1994, has passed in the Senate and is now awaiting passage in the House of Representatives. It is our opinion that these additions and administrative changes will aid significantly in the protection of these unique and priceless "scenic, historical, archeological, environmental, ecological, wildlife, cultural, scientific, educational, and recreational" resources that are "used and enjoyed by millions of Americans." *

*Report 103-165, Senate Calendar #248

The
LANDSCAPE
Part One

Golden eagle tracks on the Eureka Dunes.

Eroded badlands below Zabriskie Point, sunrise.

The pool at Badwater reflects the Black Mountains.

First light on the dunes at Mesquite Flat.

The curious "moving" rocks in Racetrack Valley.

The kaleidoscope of color at Artists Palette.

Death Valley seen from Aguereberry Point, high in the Panamints.

Salt formations on the floor of Death Valley.

Grasses and bluffs border Upper Salt Creek.

Detail of a backlit California fan palm. 22

Desertgold and badlands near Golden Canyon.

Cluster of Cottontop cactus near Teakettle Junction.

25 The eroded badlands near the head of Golden Canyon and Telescope Peak.

The salt pan of Death Valley seen from Dantes View.   26

Arrowroot in dawn's glow, Devils Cornfield.

Tin Mountain and cinder fields near Ubehebe Crater.   28

Sunrise, Mesquite Flat dunes.

DENIZENS
&
DREAMERS

Prospector weathervane at Scottys Castle, dusk.

Sidewinder rattlesnake tracks crossing Mesquite Flat Dunes. Desert bighorn ram at sunrise.

Spiral staircase at Scottys Castle.

Speckled rattlesnake in the Panamint Mountains.

Chuckawalla in the Panamint Mountains.   34

The ruins of Ashford Mill near the southern end of Death Valley.

Wagon & wheel from a "Twenty Mule Team" at Harmony Borax Works.

Abandoned vehicles in Tie Canyon adjacent to Scottys Castle.

Charcoal kilns in Wildrose Canyon.   38

Abandoned wagon-wheels near Rhyolite, Nevada.

The Watchtower at Scottys Castle in late afternoon light.   40

Desertgold, Harmony Borax Works, and Telescope Peak.

Teakettle Junction.

Coyote & creosote bush.

Wallpaper of old announcements found at an abandoned mine. 44

Petroglyphs of Bighorn sheep.

The
LANDSCAPE
Part Two

The intimacy of Marble Canyon.

Formations in the salt pan near Badwater, late afternoon.   47   Mesquite Flat dunes & the Panamint Range, early morning.

Wind-blown patterns in the sand, early morning.   48

Telescope Peak reflected in the pool at Badwater, dawn.

Darwin Falls in the Argus Range.

The "narrows" of Titus Canyon in the Grapevine Mountains.

Manly Beacon glowing in late afternoon light.

Tucki Mountain reflected in a salt pool, sunrise.

Striated rock in Mosaic Canyon.

Sensuous forms found in the dunes at Mesquite Flat.

Date palms at Furnace Creek Ranch.

The Grandstand & Ubehebe Peak, Racetrack Valley.

Ubehebe Crater reflects the glowing light of sunset. 58

Jagged salt pinnacles of the Devils Golf Course.

Telescope Peak (11,049'), the highest point in the park.

Late-afternoon on the dunes at Mesquite Flat.

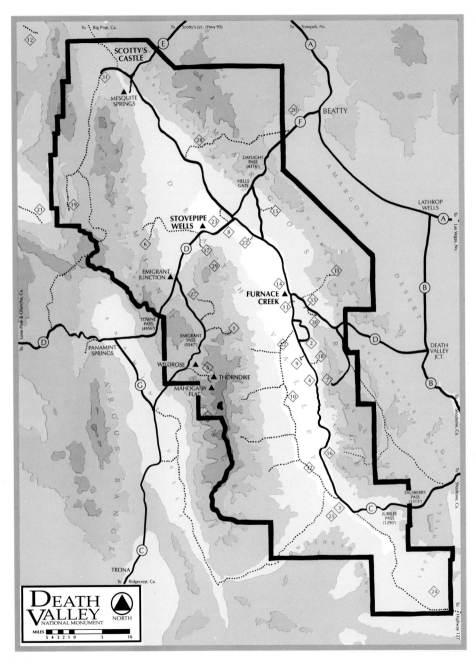

DEATH VALLEY

POINTS of INTEREST

1. Aguereberry Point (6,433-feet)
2. Artists Drive
3. Ashford Mill
4. Badwater Pool (-279.8-feet)
5. Charcoal Kilns
6. Cottonwood Canyon
7. Dantes View (5,475-feet)
8. Devils Cornfield
9. Devils Golf Course
10. Eagle Borax Works
11. Echo Canyon
12. Eureka Dunes National Natural Landmark
13. Golden Canyon
14. Harmony Borax Works
15. Keane Wonder Mine & Mill
16. Mormon Point
17. Mosaic Canyon
18. Natural Bridge
19. Racetrack Valley (3,708-feet)
20. Rhyolite (3,678-feet)
21. Saline Valley
22. Salt Creek
23. Sand Dunes (Mesquite Flat)
24. Saratoga Spring
25. Shoreline Butte (648-feet)
26. Telescope Peak (11,049-feet)
27. Skidoo
28. Titus Canyon
29. Tucki Mtn. (6,732-feet)
30. Twenty Mule Team Canyon
31. Ubehebe Crater
32. West Side Drive
33. Zabriskie Point (710-feet)

ACCOMODATIONS

WITHIN THE PARK

Fred Harvey, Inc.
P.O. Box 187
Death Valley, CA 92328
(619) 786-2345 (Furnace Creek Inn & Ranch)
(619) 786-2387 (Stove Pipe Wells Village)

NEAR THE PARK*

Baker, Ca.	113 Miles
Barstow, Ca.	175 Miles
Beatty, Nv.	42 Miles
Las Vegas, Nv.	140 Miles
Lone Pine, Ca.	108 Miles
Ridgecrest, Ca.	119 Miles
Shoshone, Ca.	57 Miles

*NOTE: Mileages are from Furnace Creek Visitor Center via the shortest paved route.

FOR MORE INFORMATION

ON DEATH VALLEY:

Superintendent
Death Valley National Monu.
Death Valley, CA 92328
(619) 786-2331

Death Valley N.H.A.
P.O. Box 188
Death Valley, CA 92328
(619) 786-3286

ON SURROUNDING PUBLIC & STATE LANDS:

U.S. Forest Service
California Region
630 Sansome St., Suite 201
San Francisco, CA 94111
(415) 556-0122

California State Park System
Dept. of Parks & Recreation
P.O. Box 942896
Sacramento, CA 94296-0001
(916) 445-6477

California Office of Tourism
P.O. Box 9278, T98
Van Nuys, CA 91409
(800) 862-2543

Bureau of Land Management
California Desert Dist. Office
1695 Spruce Street
Riverside, CA 92507
(714) 351-6394

BE PREPARED

A little planning in advance is always a good idea for the traveler. The organizations listed here will be happy to provide you with information on room reservations, campsite availability, seasonal weather patterns, hiking and wilderness permits, road conditions & vehicle size restrictions (especially motorhomes), emergency numbers, etc. This information can not only save you precious time while on vacation (always too short!), but will also help you better understand and appreciate your chosen destination.

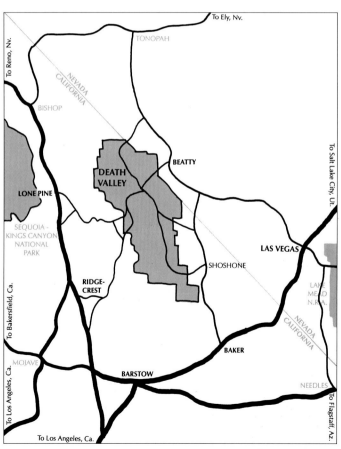

PHOTOGRAPHIC CREDITS

Larry Angier (Image West): 34.
Frank Balthis: 31-right.
Barbara A. Brundege: 6.
Carr Clifton: 47-left.
Michael Collier: 7,44.
Ed Cooper: 39,60.
Terry Donnelly (Dembinsky Assoc.): 19.
Jack W. Dykinga: 49.
Carolyn Fox (Image West): 33.
Jeff Francis: 29.
Craig Fucile: 53.
Jeff Gnass: 11,52.
Fred Hirschmann: 14,30,32.
Lewis Kemper: 31-left.
Gary Ladd: 61.
William Neill: 15-left,16,21,24,28,48,Back Cover.
Jeff Nicholas: 8,9,15-right,17,26,35,37,56,57,58.
Pat O'Hara: 22,42,59.
Chuck Place: 36.
Kurt Rhody: 12,18,38.
John Mark Stewart: 27,43,50.
Jim Stimson: 10,46.
Larry Ulrich: Front Cover,2,3-left & right,20,23,25,40,41,
47-right,51.
John Ward: 54.
Jim Wilson: 45.
Art Wolfe: 55.

CREDITS

All Death Valley Maps by Jeff Nicholas.
Book Design by Jeff Nicholas.
Photo Editor: Jeff Nicholas.
Text Editor: Nicky Leach
Printing coordinated by TWP, Ltd., Berkeley, Ca.
Printed in Singapore, 1994.

SUGGESTED READING

Austin, Mary. *The Land of Little Rain*. (1903). Albuquerque, NM: University of New Mexico Press. 1974.

Clark, Bill. *Death Valley: The Story Behind the Scenery*. (1989). Las Vegas, NV: KC Publications. 1992.

Collier, Michael. *An Introduction to the Geology of Death Valley*. Death Valley, CA: Death Valley Natural History Association. 1990.

Cornett, James W. *Death Valley National Monument: A Pictorial History*. (1986). Santa Barbara, CA: Albion Press. 1993.

Foster, Lynne. *Adventuring in the California Desert*. San Francisco, CA: Sierra Club Books. 1987.

Kirk, Ruth. *Exploring Death Valley*. (1956). Stanford, CA: Stanford University Press. 1981.

Larson, Peggy. *The Deserts of the Southwest*. San Francisco, CA: Sierra Club Books. 1977.

Schad, Jerry. *California Deserts*. Helena, MT: Falcon Press. 1988.

Van Dyke, John C. *The Desert*. (1901). Salt Lake City, UT: Peregrine Smith, Inc. 1980.

The Death Valley Natural History Association, one of many non-profit organizations chartered by Congress to aid the National Parks and Monuments, is an excellent source of affordably priced guides, pamphlets, and books. Their publications may be found in the sales areas of the Visitor Centers or by contacting them directly:

Death Valley Natural History Association
P.O. Box 188
Death Valley, CA 92328